sean burn

sean was a jessie kesson literary fellow at moniack mhor, scotlands writing centre, 2016. part of graeaes first year of 'write to play' scheme developing disabled / deaf writers, including a placement at the royal court theatre and mentoring from Selma Dimitrijevic. third full-length collection of poetry – *is that a bruise or a tattoo* still available from shearsman.

previous full-length plays include *cutter* (half moon theatre [time out's play of the year for young people], *ghost-tag* (edinburgh fringe), *sweet* (ctc), *taking the blood of butterflies* (oval house theatre), *voices* (pegasus youth theatre), & *next swan down the river might be black* (gobscure national tour, published by Aurora Metro).

last full-length play *collector of tears* toured nationally by gobscure, was north-east play of the year (British Theatre Guide), and was published by Aurora Metro.

First published in the UK in 2019 by Aurora Metro Publications Ltd.
67 Grove Avenue, Twickenham, TW1 4HX
www.aurorametro.com   info@aurorametro.com

joey © 2019 Sean Burn
explosives with love © 2019 Sean Burn
Cover image © 2019 bish – picturesbybish.com
Production: Peter Fullagar
With many thanks to: Marina Tuffier, Didem Uzum, Maja Florczak

All rights are strictly reserved.

For rights enquiries including performing rights, please contact the publisher: rights@aurorametro.com

No part of this publication may be reproduced, stored in or introduced into a retrieval system, or transmitted in any form, or by any means (electronic, mechanical, photocopying, recording or otherwise) without the prior permission of the publisher. Any person who does any unauthorised act in relation to this publication may be liable to criminal prosecution and civil claims for damages.

This paperback is sold subject to the condition that it shall not, by way of trade or otherwise, be lent, resold, hired out, or otherwise circulated without the publisher's prior consent in any form of binding or cover other than that in which it is published and without a similar condition being imposed on the subsequent purchaser.

Printed in the UK by 4edge Printers, Essex.
ISBNs:
978-1-912430-37-6 (print)
978-1-912430-38-3 (ebook)

joey

and

explosives with love

by

sean burn

AURORA METRO BOOKS

contents

acknowledgements and tour 6

cast and creatives 9

biographies 10

the play: *joey* 15

explosives with love 43

massive thanks to selma / greyscale for building teamjoey to support these writings.

and to all yu joeys too – some yet to come – keep up the love & rage

A New Wolsey Theatre testing ground commission produced by gobscure in association with Greyscale, embarking on a preview tour in June 2019, the play will be performed in english and British Sign Language:

Queens Hall, Hexham – 6th June
Pulse Festival, Ipswich – 7th June
ARC Stockton – 12th June
Northern Stage, Newcastle upon Tyne – 13th-15th June

The project is supported by ACE, Northern Stage, Andrew Lloyd Webber Foundation, Regional Theatre Young Director Scheme, Live Theatre and PULSE.

this script is being published before the play tours so might vary slightly from the performed version

www.joeytheplay.com

cast and creatives

Cast Faye Alvi
Scott Turnbull

Director Selma Dimitrijevic
Sound Design Matthew Tuckey
Assistant Director Sarah Gonnet
Associate Producer Chloe Stott
Creative BSL Consultant Brian Duffy
Photo and Digital Design picturesbybish.com
Behind the Scenes Videos Danielle Giddins

cast and creative team biographies

Faye Alvi – Performer

Faye is an experienced Theatre and Performance Interpreter and has spent the past 10 years working in North East regional theatres, TV, Music Festivals and Arenas. Faye is a CODA (Child of Deaf Adults) who has always had a passion for using BSL as an art form in Interpreted theatre & bi-lingual productions. She uses her cultural knowledge, language and performance skills to make theatre accessible for D/deaf audiences. She is experienced across genres, from children's plays to working with classical and more contemporary, experimental theatre. Prior to qualifying as an Interpreter in 2007, Faye trained in Musical Theatre and has a Performing Arts degree. She is also a classically trained singer and has performed alongside Peter Karrie *(Phantom of the Opera)*.

Scott Turnbull – Performer

Scott Turnbull is an actor and theatre maker from Teesside. His theatre company, The SMOG, creates funny, interesting and absurd theatre for audiences looking for an alternative and entertaining night out.

He was chosen by The Independent as 'One to Watch' in 2011 and was awarded North-East Actor of the Year by The North East Journal 2012.

Scott's theatre credits include *The SMOG* (Northern Stage/ARC) *Where do all the dead pigeons go?* (Northern Stage/Greyscale/ARC) *Gods are fallen and all safety gone* (Greyscale) *Get Santa* (Northern Stage) *The Rubber Room*

(The Old Vic), *The Machine Gunners* (Polka Theatre), *Apples* (Northern Stage), *The Tempest* (KG Productions), *Book of Beasts* (Catherine Wheels Theatre Company), *Hansel and Gretel* (Northern Stage), *Heartbreak Soup* (Empty Space Productions), *A Christmas Carol* (Northern Stage) and *How Many Miles to Basra?* (The West Yorkshire Playhouse). His television credits include *Little Bastard, Wolfblood, The Royal Today, The Bill* and *Byker Grove*.

Selma Dimitrijevic – Director

Selma is a director and writer, and artistic director of Greyscale. Her work has played in venues such as Dundee Rep, Traverse, Tron, Northern Stage, Manchester Exchange, Hull Truck, Theatre Royal Bath, Almeida and international festivals. As a writer she specialises in radical adaptations of classic texts and her plays and adaptations have been performed in over a dozen countries around the world. She has translated a number of major English contemporary novels into Croatian and as a librettist she worked at Royal Opera House (*Berenice*), Aldeburgh Festival (*To See the Invisible*) , South Bank Centre *(Zatopek!)* and Opera North (*Big Bums*). She also works as a dramaturg, most recently on Sting's large scale musical *The Last Ship* (UK and Canada tour).

Matthew Tuckey – Sound Designer

Matthew is a sound designer working in theatre, music and video as well as creating independent pieces of sound art. Matthew's roots as a creative are in experimental music production and devised theatre. He regularly collaborates with other artists and theatre makers who are driven by a love of storytelling and immersive experiences.

Sarah Gonnet – Assistant Director

Sarah is a multi-media writer and artist from the North-East of England. She makes work in a number of forms. She is currently developing a play about the history of women in film, with support from Arts Council England; and a piece of immersive artwork about Louise Bourgeois, with support from New Writing North. She is the author of many plays that look at both mental illness and feminism, including *Word Salad* which was performed as part of Alphabetti Theatre's award winning *The Rooms*. She has previously published a book of poetry, *Voices*.

Eva Collins Alonso – Stage Manager

Eva is a Stage Manager, Production Manager & LX Technician working in theatre contexts in Spain & the UK. She studied at the University of Bedfordshire and Royal Central School of Speech & Drama, and trained as a technician at Northern Stage & Almadraba Teatro (Alicante). She has worked at Omnibus Theatre & Arts Depot (London) but her favourite is touring with companies such as The SMOG, Lost Disk, Rhiannon Faith, Worklight Theatre & Gustavo Dias-Ballejo.

Chloe Stott – Associate Producer

Chloe is a theatre producer based in the North East. She has worked extensively with Alphabetti Theatre since 2016, training as a producer under the guidance of Artistic Director Ali Pritchard. With Alphabetti she has produced

The Frights (2016), *Bacon Knees & Sausage Fingers* (2016 & 2019), *The Rooms* (2016), *How Did We Get To This Point?* (2016), *Walter & Wilfred* (2017 & 2018) and *The Christmas Cabaret* (2017 & 2018). She is currently working as Producer for Sarah Gonnet's new play, *The Female Gaze*.

Brian Duffy – Creative BSL Consultant

Duffy has always been interested in visually accessible theatre. He co-created the sign language sitcom *Small World*, as well as acted in it and several shorts and most recently a theatre production of Sarah Kane's *4:48 Psychosis*. Worked as BSL creative with the RSC for their recent three productions. Secretly moonlights as The Mime, a pro-wrestler.

joey

1:
1981 c.e. (common era)
shops/carehome – sean

carehome head sends psycho-us downtown to collect bread only its still in oven & bakers dont want us hangin round so we nips next door where they have everythin

– screws / sticky numbers / glitter in ruby & silver / seeds for flowers & veg & birds

theres even cartoon eyes that roll as psycho-us pass today discovers metal-rings for fingers in pirate – butterfly – crow

we reach out & take rings for spaz & dumbo – our two best friends – our only friends – our chosen family

in heart-thump we tug pirate ring free for our friend dumbo

more heart-thump as we curl fist around crow for our other friend spaz

pocket both rings which shout *here we are daddy, here we are*

gonna be jumped by shopkeeper for thievery but gotta have these for our family even if we get sent some place even worse

shopkeeper arrives as were near blackin out

dont faint or yu'll bring this display down. outside. now

& he opens door where social-work-teacher-coppers rise up laughin

... only they dont...

& somehow we make it back to carehome

where head ov homes face falls cos were not carryin his bread

so he fetches his cane, takes his time

seize this chance

wink for our family ov dumbo & spaz to slide over fast

& then we whip those nicked rings onto their fingers & pirate-dumbo & crow-spaz kiss our psycho-face

carehome head returns – flexes cane

– pants down – touch yr toes – oggy oggy oggy oi oi oi

– is everyone shoutin or is this memory?

way things bleed in our mind meanin were never quite sure

shit on carehome heads cane before droppin to the ground

fallin, we think how much time will we lose this time around?

steppin out ov time

    bomb blast. ripped from light. that silence after
    those settlins ov dust

    at last findin yu's two spaz & dumbo – family grinnin unstoppable
    us three lovin&ragin – no-one will steal our time together

joey

before the explosion? no. there is always after

steppin back into time

1981s one summer long ov riotin – some ov the burn is right outside toxteth-handsworth-wolverhampton-coventry-leicester-derby-moss-side-woolwich-leeds-ellesmere port-luton-sheffield-portsmouth-preston-newcastle-upon-tyne-southampton-nottingham-bedford-edinburgh-aldershot-stockport-blackburn-huddersfield-reading-chester-bradford & high wycombe – where the fucks that?

black folks ov coventry fightin back against incomin skinheads

asians battlin nazis for southall

cops clobberin brixton black & blue cos they find no molotovs

bobby sands & then nine more die in the maze prison hunger-strike

unemployment rockets – two point four million – two point five million –

two point six million

norman tebbit shouts *get on yr bikes* & the con party stand & cheer

orphan-scum gettin kicked out soon enough

our scraps in plastic bags preparin us for the nick – street or loony-bin

a royal weddin is set for july

prince charles – princess d-d-d-d-d-d-d-die!

their satanic majestys'll see to that once she's too fat or suicidal
– divorce first or straight for the kill?
prince charles likin 'em young, the royals always do
all ov us in care are way younger than princess di-di-di
the royals are givin us somethin *spesh-ull* so *come down in yr best*
last time we got lined up this way outsiders handed over colour tele
but the lesson always is pay-off after – blow-jobs after
– just werent expectin us to try bitin their knobs off
& so were all lined up again
the youngest brushed their teeth, still no gettin it
royals representative shakes hands with staff, moves down the line
we drop a curtsey & head ov home throws fist at us
royals-representative flinches – drops handbag – make-up spillin
we pocket scarlet lippie while dumbo nicks nail-scissors
spaz looks to pile on in only order gets restored
& royal mugs are handed out right down the line
a loyal-royal toast to prince charles & his beautiful bride – all pray
& then our most beautiful spaz spits the words that turn all around
gods prey? yu's are the ones preyin on us
which is why gods fucked off & she aint comin back

raisin & smashin weddin mugs while singin from
stiff little fingers suspect device

2:
1981 c.e. school – sean

waitin for school-bell to let us inside is like waitin for a knife

todays stabbin – *yr to welcome the new english teacher*
most times we fight back with golf balls up their exhaust
only this one plays punk for poetry!

givin us such words & worlds – sweet fuck yu's all
beats instead ov beaten – what weve ached for

voices ov protest & ov protection from swansea to soweto

delta blues from mississippi to the mekong

orchestras from germany, saxes from the states, klezmer from all over

pipes from ireland to spain, percussion from india to nigeria

the drag ov needle across record – hum ov amps – tapes squeal

john peel across the airwaves with that international ov guitar – bass – drum – how we ached for these banshee-siren-songbirds

nothin stops spaz from singin out but our dumbo got silenced long ago

truly, she's no spoken in all those years since we first met

sure she shows us her scars on arms & back some nights

& her nicked scissors swear back at all who spit on her golden skin but her lips are always locked except when openin in kiss-chasins kiss-chase is sposed to be lads forcin theirselves on lasses while adults look the other way – but our kiss-chases different!

us bein lad & our dumbo a lass means the two ov us together cornerin others always makes it 'wrong' unless its our beamin spaz

course our kiss-chasin dont actually kiss anyone –

we just get in close enough to see the rage beautiful across their faces!

singin chorus from **stiff little fingers** *nobody's hero*

our punk-poet-teachers always says keep runnin with this love&rage

& then they spin another record – 33rpm – 33 revolutions per minute

life-lessons from them & john peel both

after another after-hours listenin session slippin out real casual

bisexuals the word yu's are all lookin for

& we three roll bi around our tongues

always known our longins but no their namins

so now we are bi always – plurals better always – bisexualities

our punk-poets the only teacher who never asks for payment

instead giftin us *make some noise – get heard – ask more questions*

& so our spaz questions repeatedly

– why preach hang nelson mandela then teach turn the other cheek?

– whys that book got french dictionary written on when it should be

dictionnaire & – excuse our french – français?

– wz edward the second king or a queen?

– yu lecture that dumbo aint true brit but prince philip is?

– biology said were all animals so yr volunteerin to be experimented on?

– saint george – what wz god smokin when she designed dragons?

– chemistry tells the names ov chemicals but no how to blow stuff up

– why teach us to play the drums quiet when theyre built for war?

– & wheres high wycombe?

steppin out ov time

after each explosion more changes

flickin the v's becomes middle-finger

cowboys & indians becomes brits against germans turns u.s.

versus commies – cops become feds, shit turns shite,

transsexual becomin transgender

& thru it all – spaz beat-never-beaten & dumbos scissor-strikins

steppin back into time

> our punk-poet teacher always says *asks more questions*
> & so spaz asks sweetly for bara brith
> this gorgeous welsh cake from next weeks cookery
> lads arent allowed to cook – instead were forced into t.d. – technical drawin – stabbed or be stabbed with wee metal compasses
> spaz is plannin to get into that cookin class & were a key ingredient
> so weve a week to nick dried fruit – self-raisin flour – brown sugar
> cinnamon – nutmeg – ginger – cloves – tea-bags – lemons
> eggs thats arent smashed & enough butter to slather all in
> finally queuin outside cookery door with all weve stolen
> only for miss to point spaz & us back over to technical drawin
> spaz keeps waftin spice-soaked fruit under her nose
> miss keeps rappin spaz with a wooden love-spoon for stayin in lasses queue only spaz bites chunks out ov love-spoon till miss sits in doorway talkin to splinters & we all step over her & into cookery
> spaz makes sure egg & sugar & flour are stirred in
> cookers fire on up so cake gets baked
> & then we all eat butter-slathered bara brith & still warm

singin from **stiff little fingers** ***nobodys heroes***

> our punk-poet teacher gifted us the right & so we question everythin
> right up till our teachers colossal stroke into that flowerbed beside playground steps

joey

tho questions continue there are no answers to their fall-fallin-fallen

dyin right in front ov us means constant storm ov rain in our eyes

right thru till day ov the memorial when we spot this unbelievable tulip dress – golden against dark times

need to wear this to show true respect!

we sort thru the dresses with shakin hands & find our size

pick up our tulip dress & edge towards store-door

only theres movement from this store-worker

each time we edge closer to the door they move too – dare we run?

only management arrives & then the coppers

in for a penny in for a pound – lead a merry dance around

– we all know yr no buyin

& they point to door

– yu have this dress in our size? were 14, a 14, a size 14

– yr upsettin other customers sir, yu'll have to leave

– sir? & besides theres no other customers

– nevertheless i must insist yu leave sir

oggy oggy oggy oi oi oi & they march us out

wish we had worn that flower dress for our punk-poet teacher

wish we'd worn that dress to see the smile split our dumbos face

wish our spaz had pissed theirself laughin at our tulip dress

& us punk-pure in rememberin

3:
1981 c.e. carehome / psychiatric hospital – sean

nights grow longer – daylight shortens – shadows are closin in

unscrew lightbulb from our bedside lamp
spit on fingers & jam 'em to socket – electrics fizzle
a second time & greater electric fizz
third time lucky?

how much time we lost before comin round on far sides ov bedroom?

– *yr a bleedin catastrophe* – head ov home bellows
oggy oi oggy oggy oi & he bodyslams us, crackin our ribs
draggin us to cortina – shotgunnin engine, jumpin red lights
roads stretch – street-lights switch on – ever been this far out before?
finally were thrown at feet ov nurses – porters – psychiatrist
spaz always said we'd end here – the loony-bin
handed medication then water & then forced to swallow
then they open our mouth to prove we have
& their non-stop questions!
eatin – sleepin – washin?

joey

yu hearin voices?

on a scale ov one to ten

eat voices – dream yr watched – washin – oggy-oggy?

voices say yr failure sleepin? better off dead? eat – oi-oi-oi!

watch yr followed – voices failed – dead off – oggy-oi-oggy-oi!

sleep-dream-watch – followed yr failure – dead-oggyoggyoi

singin from **stiff little fingers** *at the edge*

just once makin ends ov ward corridor & findin this thick glass door

thru this we glimpse film-set where deep-space acid-blood lurks

oi! get thrown down – arse-needled – dragged back

– yu need punishin. we all agree on that – illegal ovcourse but who ever listens to wee fuckers like yu?

unilateral e.c.t. & both electrodes to same side ov head – seizure!

bilateral e.c.t. – electrodes either side head – seizure!

bi-frontal e.c.t. with electrodes between – seizure!

steppin out ov time

before the explosion?

weve forgotten ... so much time stolen
so much time is stolen ... explosions steal so much
strugglin to keep golden dumbo, grinnin spaz in mind

... & after?

steppin back into time

    psychiatrists war-talk is pure torture
    & hospital-meds jitter us more
    plus weve no more ribs left to crack
    so we gets booted back

    carehome staff gob over us as we walk their corridor refusin to cry

    dumbo holds staff back with scissors
    spaz takes our shakin hands
(doin this) & we draw this giant heart with nicked lippie
    write inside the giant crimson heart
    spaz-dumbo-psycho

4:
1981 c.e. school – sean

school days bleeds. which workbooks gonna be ripped from us next?

only somethin hangs over today like crows before storm

spaz is even later arrivin than usual – most times theyre here for lunch

but today its just us & dumbo pushin grey spuds thru grey gravy

burnt sausages gobbed over us by dogs-ov-war sittin next table across before we all unite in flingin discs ov grey carrot at grey teachers

lunch ends & we head for playground where we find spaz pacin

weve seen that stare in photos ov war

spaz pushes thru everyone

knockin mugs ov sweet tea out teachers hands

finally spirallin to dead centre while flickin the v's

our heart goin out as spaz beats drums ov war

– *blue peter last night with joey deacon – werent it great!*

mental – subnormal – spaz-spacker-mongol – wheelchair joey – tongue-tied deacon – stutter-splutter joey

only joey deacon writes a book, gets on tele

he even gets to travel & live in a bungalow with his mates

(more flickin the v's) well fuck the lotta yu's –

yu's will all call me joey, ma names joey, i'm joey from now on

& with that name change – everythin changes
nothin can ever be the same again
our spaz becomes joey, we become sean, & dumbo is zehra
joeys unstoppable – shoutin & silencin school bell
sean & zehra now – both ov us move to joeys side – ball our fists
we three havin stood back to back waitin so many times before
this time playground only stares like meat before teachers run, their kids followin
joey now heads for chestnut tree where fires hollowed grooves
sudden big-kid puttin finger to lips – *were joey-she-he*
& so zehra & us – we calls 'em joey-she-he now on

they gave lou reed e.c.t cos he wz bi.
dont let 'em give yu

& joey repeats

they gave lou reed e.c.t cos he wz bi.
dont let 'em give yu

& leanin in closer – we smooch – we smooch a while
joey she-he runnin hands down our face

steppin out ov time

before the explosion? no! there is always after
each smooch – blow – stroke – beatin – caress – skin rememberin

& always zehra & joey – long may yu's run, long may yu's run

steppin back into time

    now zehra strokes joey as they smooch
    & now joey she-he places that knackered cassette ov stiff little fingers live into zehras hands & folds our fingers over it too
    joey she-he squeezin songs ov life into us both
    now joey runs at fencin, fingers hookin wire in graceful ascent
    never lookin back, that drop beyond
    joey she-he in the wind, disappeared, gone

    that rain in our eyes? been rainin ever since

singin from **stiff little fingers** *suspect device*

5:
leadin to 1991 c.e. record shop – sean

joey read the future & flew

but by first handin over that precious cassette ov stiff little fingers live

joey saw a future for us too –

we seize that future – dive thru record shops doorway ov darkest red

& just like in the song we find a home not a house

records – tee-shirts – zines – cassettes – fliers – badges – magazines

con party wear hang nelson mandela badges

but we find a home among anti-apartheid & other human rights – feminisms – queernesses – earth first defendin all species

for five year we put out new releases

& we write to this amazin person named v who writes back

5 year ov love-letters wingin in from v in thessaloniki, northern greece

southern europe – 1981 thru to 1986

photos ov their long black hair & smoulderin eyes makin us buckle!

record shop was sanctuary – encyclopedia – home

never expected the delicious sweet lovin embarrassment ov them savin our earnins across those five years to pay for v to fly in

so we could be face-to-facin, in love fallin & fallen

joey

over&over, over no out – fuuuuucckk!

yu are family v – knowin this soon as we hold each other

v arrivin – armin & warmin us with love

is the very first to hear our writins

v is beside us thru every gig – demo – riotin

v gives freedom to struggle on

lovin & ragin in v's arms & how!

& now our only family v since joey flew & then zehra wz permanently silenced!

v wz beside us as we raged across 1986 givin zehras 18 year ov ash back to her beloved rivers – tees, trent, wysyg

at least zehra found freedom out on those white-waters

powerin down rapids, ridin stoppers, shootin weirs

even tho p.t.o. – please turn over – wz gaffer-taped to bottom ov kayak

zehra never capsized – even their kayak wz called a dancer

freezin waters finally allowin her to come alive

goosebumps livin with us forever

moments stolen from that storm ov holdin other kids together

zehra tryin always to save lives in that endless incomin

we would-ov stroked her bloodied hands longer

at least on those white-waters zehra found freedom

1986 : hell ov a year – livin & dyin both

6:
1991 c.e. street – sean

what time is love? finally charts – welcome to 1991
klf also sing *justified & ancient* & *its grim up north*
& a british scientist creates a web linkin computers across the world
our lads join the yanks in bombin baghdad
downing streets windows get blown in by i.r.a. bombs
& con party – in power for ever – throw more folks on the dole & go up in the polls
leeds-cardiff-handsworth-dudley-tyneside all riot
oxford – just twenty miles from high wycombe as crows fly – joins in
what time is love? is no just in the charts
its v & us bakin greek bread together
stirrin honey into warm water & then foamin up yeast
addin greek olive oil – salt – wholemeal flour in
throw in fried onions – greek olives – rosemary
knead & leave to rise & then bake
& when all is golden to tear on in
before bathin together & makin great ragin love

only one day crashes & burns – v's voice crackin
– *theres somethin we have to tell – cant keep it in any longer*
all but passin out in panic-attackin
– *dont leave us – dont leave – dont*
v's – *were no leavin yu! yu & us together always. & in all-ways. now weve always been no-questions-cool*

joey

with yu bein bi, well now were needin yu no-questions-cool too

& v waves hands over groin sayin

– this meat never will be us – am settin date for it to all be gone – our real birth day... jes need to face those demons back in thessaloniki one last – make 'em hear who we really are

we reply by wavin v's groin away

– wz never yu as lad / lass we fell for v – always & in all ways head-over-heels for y smoulderin eyes – dark-coffee – bread-bakin – bi means our skin together on those north sea beaches, that tingle ov love, nothin else matters

go make great ragin love before climbin from our bath

(doin this) & smashin screen out abandoned tele

& draggin this empty screen in wheelie-bin alongside chairs

& as pedestrian crossin beep-beeps – beep-beeps – beep-beeps

we wheelie-bin to middle – place tele on – settle in to watch

drivers honk-honkin before coppers eventual – *yu cant sit here*

– ssssh – its blue peter – edge-yu-cay-shun-all!

– yu cant sit middle this crossin all day

– we wanna watch tele all day long!

their finger-wag means we slow-wheel off

& then go sit the next crossin down. & the next. its a long road!

& with v's coffee coursin we love & we rage in tellin ov joey & zehra con party mayov outlawed 'promotin homosexuality' with clause 28 but yu'll never stop our bi-trans love-ins!

this whole time weve been worryin on v's final visit to thessaloniki crash & burn once more when v waves groin away &

– be gone one month only, make 'em hear who we truly are –

then we can be whole, celebrate a birth day, share yr surname

one week drags two, two drags three, three draggin four

now the s.w.p. – socialist workers party – always hated us for bein bi,

v for bein trans, & both ov us for no carryin their placards on our protests

& now this one s.w.p. member who always attacked v & us for readin poetry together proposes coffee?

walk away but he follows – cant shake shit off shoes a whole hour until

– party bosses have declared we are all theoretically bisexual...

we er need to understand oppression better... yu couldnt er... ?

theoretical bisexuals?

it finally dawns

joey

– yr wantin us to fuck yu?

he nods nervously

– what about v?

– he neednt

– he?

– she

– she?

– dont need to know

– so if we fuck yr arse – no imagination – yu'll fuck off?

he's prepared to better understand pain by takin one for his party – gettin fucked is politics only, no pleasure!

v will howl with laughter when we tell about fuckin with this s.w.p. & so we bark – *bend over*

arsehole drops trews – moonin traffic spinnin off the roundabout

& in our best punk we serenade his white arse – literally sing-shout-howl stiff little fingers at his open arse – just no too close!

singin from **stiff little fingers** *wait & see*

six weeks in & this telegrams delivered

body found stop suspicious circumstances stop yr name on stop friend question-mark please contact

steppin out ov time

there wz the explosion... but... before... wz there a before?

yu cant be dead v, yu cant be gone
how will we remember yr smoulderin eyes v?
how can we remember yr fire burnin, yr lovin-rage?
there is no after this explosion

steppin back into time

v's dyin hurls meteors which crash species to extinction
libraries burn – all music ends – universes fold back in on themselves
let this universe fold back in on itself. & the next universe. & the next

in emptiness we crap into carrier-bags, then walk out carryin them
stay under tree where crows nest only social work hunts us down
we hurl bag on bag ov crap at them but our arms tire
& then the rain hits our eyes
& we get arse-needled – drug-dragged – the whole way back

over slow months arrivin at ends ov that wards corridor
the familiar thick glass door with deep-space acid-blood beyond

joey

finally to unlock door with thieved key – free again

only minds so blown we can only focus on nickin teddies – penguins – dolls – whales – one crow

our fingers cannot be unlocked from grippin those cuddlies even as were dragged back to hospital, dragged down corridors, dragged to ward

oggy oi oggy oi oggy oi oggy oggy oggy oi oi oi

the last ov our energy arcs armfuls ov teddies – penguins – dolls

– whales across wards beds

keepin hold ov that lone crow as we fall for ever

7:
future (around 2025 c.e.)
- joey aged mid-50s

after leapin from that wire fence & disappearin
– joeys travelled far & wide

(showin) wearin that crow ring – carryin those scissors across forty years

sometimes hidin in plain sight

joeys been growin & growlin

slowly puzzlin things out

joey never did mind gettin called slow

joey got told about merched beca – rebecca riots – way back

somethin about folks across south wales two hundred years before

puttin on frocks to step against clergy-merchants-army & smash tollgates made joey grin

way more choke-holds in supply chains now

so many possible futures to be written in 2025 and beyond

so joey frocks n rocks up – ready now to rewrite this future

offerin apple stars

this joey cuts apples in half *wrong-ways* & then hands out these stars

this joey hands one apple star to orphan bein nicked for lyin in the road

once inside police cell split this fruit in two – two halves make a whole so climb thru that hole to escape

joey

the look on coppers faces! the smile on hers!
that joke always crackin zehra & sean wide

offerin roses

this joeys smile when given kurdish roses by freedom fighter & her lass!

so many have fought for rojava, so many fight alongside the kurds

this joey smiles wider when those freedom fighters show how thorns ov kurdish roses defend the bud against attack so it gets to flower

the kurds hand out actual roses to teach self-defence?!

joey plants freedoms roses everywhere

offerin lipstick

for valentines day this joey steals black & red lipsticks for all

for april fools this joey steals clock-hands outta schools

on may days this joey dances with communists-anarchists-poles

this joey writes *thank god were atheists* across every cathedrals visitors book

this joey spray-paints *our dream jobs dreamin* across a hundred job centres

this joey throws psychiatric notes & psychiatrists into rivers trent-tees-wysyg

this joey rolls marbles under politicians feet shoutin *yu'v lost these!*

this joey shares fruitcake, rewilds lynxes, smashes in every screen they find this joey commutes on space-hoppers

this joey sticks stamps upside down on every envelope

this joey obeys the law exactly – slowin everythin right down

this joey asks police officers if they can be be done for impersonatin a police officer? they drive off. fast

this joey cut ties off anyone who would be boss

this joey pours red wine down white frocks at racist weddins

this joey feeds laxative chocolate to an entire towns dignitaries – m-mmm!

this joeys cookery lessons teach kids how custard powders an explosive

this joey celebrates guy fawkes – the most honest person in parliament – by lightin up a horizon with fireworks lorry

this joey smashes glasses outta psychiatrists hands screamin half full still?

makin shadows

each hiroshima day – 6th august – this joey paints atomic shadows across a new town – on nagasaki day – 9th august – this joey does it again

with rainbow laces

this joey pins suffragette colours to racehorses

this joey gives rainbow laces to every football team

this joey dresses as santa & then tells kids in-store all the toys are free

this joey writes *vive la republique* on the plaster ov the kings broken arm this joey stands besides politicians, every time their gob opens, *cuckoooo!*

this joey serves magic mushroom tea at newspapers daily conferences & makes sure they drink

this joey marks down the price of cremation caskets and opens windows for the dyin

this joey eats & breathes fire & walks thru flames

& everywhere joey goes they shout when were dreams first stolen?

when were yr dreams first stolen?

the end

explosives with love

ideally performed to limited audiences (8 – 12) led to carlas cell and told the 'rules' having had hand-held metal-detectors waved over them

soundscape

monologue takes place against a pre-recorded soundscape conveying oppression (atmosphere not keys, footsteps etc) before finally moving towards liberation (curlews matter!). as gobscure, we are acclaimed broadcast / exhibited sound-artist and would deliver soundscape too

film

a 'horizon' breaks the cells walls towards the end and we see those curlews. (we are also acclaimed film-maker and will deliver this film)

kathy boudin: *i lost my way. twelve years underground, isolation, different names, a lost self. i had arrived at a deeply wrong way ov responding to social problems. prison lies at the end ov a road taken. ... now more than twenty years in prison, i share with other women daily issues ov parenting, education, and health. i have turned sixty. i think about how do we protect our planet.'*

location

prison cell in the south-lands

carla

female. fifty. queer. environmental activist ov the northlands. mother.

carla gave son a snow globe
(showing) showed him how to shake it up slow
sayin – said – this is the land us gotta fight for
for now yr to stay and play son, enjoy the snow so
us'll be back – soon son, soon

and now? fifteen year on
and its bastard hard caged in prison-law
wasn't meant to be like this
but they know how to turn up the heat
this box they've put us in
this metal and concrete box
this mental box ov key and camera
this spied on box, spied-upon box,
box within a box – us all are in, jailed and jailers
how they shake it up
only no like ours sons snowy globe

was declared unfit to be at large
unfit to breathe that northlands air
unfit to parent, unfit to love, unfit to alive-alive-oh
and all us did was clad explosives to steel-pilin and concrete
and us all – in our own ways – handle detonators
who hasn't felt that surge ov anger once they burn yr lands
choke yr woman off as they rape yu down
they know that explosive surge with their mother ov all bombs

explosives with love

their 'collateral damage', their 'blue-on-blue', their 'psy-ops'
cruise and patriot and minutemen
carpet-bombin – paisley or wolsey mass destruction sir?
mass distraction, generalissimo bollocks
about time yu learned yu cant always win

changin names, nom de guerre, goin underground
havin son with another woman long choked down
son, miss yu so – was only wantin to preserve the northlands
woman mixin acetone with phosphate, grindin it down
plantin tubes, wirin all up, buryin command wires
and – defyin the maternal instinct
as if yu cant plant explosives with love
as if wirin it up just so cant be tenderness
as if violence cannot be out ov desire
as if women are not allowed to believe
the whole ov life before that one act erased
everythin weve done since isnt accepted as rehabilitation
nothin else weighs in their balance
those lands: that north – will us be returnin?
sometimes jailor spits in our face
sometimes the whisper is parole ...

best not to torture yrself too long or too hard with hope

as interrogator

with which centre ov revolution did yu identify?

did yu adopt tactics flowin from foreign principles?

how did yu carry out yr commitments underground?

do yu deny receivin communiqué readin

the clash ov civilizations is a romantic term. forget mediaeval horsemen: expect instead a fistfight with vodka bottles in a plywood bar?

do yu see yrself as a fistfighter?

do yu drink vodka?

do yu see the west – civilization – as plywood bar?

did yu harvest sugar-cane in cuba?

did yu plant coffee in nicaragua?

show solidarity with rojava?

would yu define yrself as internationalist in perspective?

have yu read mary wollstonecraft?

do yu whistle the red flag?

take bob dylans lyrics seriously?

have yu dropped lsd?

do yu subscribe to chaos theory?

would yu stand in the way ov catastrophe bonds?

do yu identify with mao's *a single spark can start a prairie fire*?

castro's *duty ov a revolutionary is to make a revolution*?

che guevaras *2, 3, many vietnams*?

prisoner will answer, goddammit

as herself

explosives with love

ultimate anger as yu pin down our woman one last
our lands mutilated, freedoms eroded – again
terra is land – that fierce lovin burn
whose terra? and whose terror?
who wouldnt fall for all the northlands have been through
my woman, scars ov yr skin – wee crescents ov yr flag
unlike those straight lines they try forcin thru the land
laughin with as yu tell – told *am no straight, am curvy*
fierce, protective, love – how us fell
they ask is there anythin yu would die for?
ask instead is there anythin for whom yu would kill?
for yu, ma fearsome love, ma fierce lovin, and then some

in that cold state
bein shown yr final box ov skin
bruises on yu – purple – yellow
nipple eye neck
fish-hooks ov flesh ripped off ov yu
am longin to stroke
achin to trace yr bruisin
instead punchin the wall
hands fucked from punchin too many walls
holes made ov yu when wantin to get hold ov yu
in sheer bloody normalness ov bleed
conquistadors ov pain – about time someone rebelled
time us done yr empires in

remember yu playin with the soft poolin wax from candles

turnin that slow-tide this way n that

dammin it with fingers – that hot slide pourin out and over skin

aah sweet pain, the bliss ov it

later those acts ov war done on yr skin

in return am wantin to fist the explosives hi

blow their bridges – retreat with our son to that other side

they didnt even allow us yr ash to scatter

in return that surge – anger-desire-love – who hasn't?

theres a fierce tenderness in handlin explosives

the clash ov civilizations is a romantic term. forget mediaeval horsemen: expect instead a fistfight with vodka bottles in a plywood bar

should be taught in schools instead ov most their shite

who hasn't wanted to torch cathedrals – parliaments – castles

blow holes in military runways and psych icu walls

they're just found in guidebooks, on postcards or map

somethin to lick besides kings head – aint real, right?

should be people, community, us care for

marx and angels, marx and angels

suit n tie – uniform – cassock makes us shake

were no monster – that bridge, concrete, was monstrous

explosives with love

not bridgin but rippin the guts out
flowin our resource out
relentless shadow flown across our great northlands
business cementin that deal
heather and blueberry concreted
raspberry cane ripped out
cliffs blasted down to new pure sand so yu can build some more
and the marsh and the marsh harrier and the marsh orchid torn
the northlands riven – driven – reived – no relief
dodgy deals-boozy backroom stitch-ups-backhanders-backslaps and slappers rented for brown-nosed masons ov land – ex-ministers directorships and sinkin their quick pricks slick into shores where us'd lain undisturbed so bloody long

terra carved up everywhere – somethin has to blow

dignitaries flown in to open that fuckin bridge
only its no bridgin, its drivin a wedge

blowin somethin is no wetdream
sweat to eyes, hands shakin, holdin yr bladder in

con – cen – trate
and
now

and all us did was topple y ache ov concrete penetratin morthlands

minders whisper in their ministers ear

secret services shittin trews as they retire all to safe distance

cameras capturin the smiles collapse alongside concrete

ever watched a skylark unfold then drag its wing over heather –

pretendin its broke to lead predators from the nest

cant see that from car windows – yu gotta look close

only yu couldn't live with landbitch chewin out yr span
so us hunted down – carrion blood shat across moor

as interrogator

were yu radicalised by the internet or yr ahem-mental-state?

internet or yr ahem-mental-state?

radicalised by the internet or

yu must … will answer

do not persist in non-compliance

who do yu think yu are?

do yu hear voices?

do yu sleep?

do yu dream in grey or blue?

explosives with love 51

are yu suicidal ... yet?
do yu believe in lizard overlords?
lick lizards as yr gateway drug?
why dya – dya even like lizards?
do yu eat meat?
would yu eat mine?
do yu want me to take my lanyard off?
why are yu takin this personally?
why have yu never learned yr times tables?

who – do – yu – think – yu – are?

carla

    the willingness ov a girl – fifteen years young

    to douse herself with petrol – set herself alight for her true state from hospital bed sayin she will do it again for kurdistan

    the burn ov fuel in lungs – sting in eyes – clag ov petrol to tongue

    preferable to terror ov state bombin yr mountains

    in intensive care sister doin her rounds
    examinin screen

tracin a monitor line which slows and stops

beep beeeep beeeeeep

what hope for teenagers from those furthest corners ov terra?

oh son, us love yu son, soon son soon

have us lost that craziness? aye
us understand so different now jan palachs forgotten
vietnam monks aflame are seen only as album cover
molotovs just another cocktail for victims ov fashion
semtex is an energy drink
and kalashnikov would rather ov invented a lawnmower

worst punishment was bein sent south
lawns and fountain at entrance to prison
gloved warders pullin back labia
what they expectin to find?

sounds ov curlew grow until the end

still a heart ov semtex pumpin within
but findin theres more than one way ov takin it apart

oh son love yu son love yu love yu soon
after fifteen year that postcard enterin ma cell

explosives with love

the curves ov land so familiar

... parole? head north. northlands

hold our teenage son as he shakes that snowglobe

in war yu cant bury yr dead – so wantin to bury our woman

then lie at peace on the rough ov pebbles

dolphins dancin the firth

whaleback mountains beyond

a scatterin ov ancient pines

orchids clingin on

the end

North-East Play Of The Year 2014
– British Theatre Guide

'and i have collected tears ever since those darkest hours of 1431. and for a hundred years i did not age.'

An epic love story told across four centuries by Sunderland-born Tanya Sealt, a woman who cannot age until she has cried. *collector of tears* is a play about history, oppression and loss.

'... a stirring, thought-provoking and uplifting piece of theatre.' – UK Theatre Network

112 pages / £8.99
978-1-906582-91-3

'you think you won't survive, but you do...'

next swan down the river might be black is a poetic and personal response to being sectioned under the mental health act.

'Sometimes poetic, often distressing.' – The Stage

56 pages / £8.99
978-1-906582-35-7

THE DIVIDED LAING by Patrick Marmion
ISBN 978-1-906582-82-1   £8.99

GRAEAE PLAYS 1: New Plays Redefining Disability selected by Dame Jenny Sealey ISBN 978-0-9536757-6-0   £12.99

SPLIT/MIXED by Ery Nzaramba
ISBN 978-1-911501-97-8   £10.99

A GIRL WITH A BOOK by Nick Wood
ISBN 978-1-910798-61-4   £12.99

THE TROUBLE WITH ASIAN MEN by Sudha Bhuchar, Kristine Landon-Smith and Louise Wallinger ISBN 978-1-906582-41-8   £8.99

SOUTHEAST ASIAN PLAYS eds. Cheryl Robson and Aubrey Mellor
ISBN 978-1-906582-86-9   £16.99

SIX PLAYS BY BLACK AND ASIAN WOMEN WRITERS ed. Kadija George
ISBN 978-0-9515877-2-0   £12.99

WOMEN OF ASIA by Asa Palomera
ISBN 978-1-906582-94-4   £7.99

HARVEST by Manjula Padmanabhan
ISBN 978-0-9536757-7-7   £6.99

I HAVE BEFORE ME A REMARKABLE DOCUMENT by Sonja Linden
ISBN 978-0-9546912-3-3   £7.99

THE IRANIAN FEAST by Kevin Dyer
ISBN 978-1-910798-93-5   £8.99

NEW SOUTH AFRICAN PLAYS ed. Charles J. Fourie
ISBN 978-0-9542330-1-3   £11.99

www.aurorametro.com